my first
word
book

Angela Wilkes

DK

DORLING KINDERSLEY

London • New York • Stuttgart

A Dorling Kindersley Book

Note to parents

My First Word Book is an entertaining picture book for you and your child to share. Your child will enjoy recognizing the colourful photographs and illustrations of everyday things. By pointing to the word labels as you name each object, you will help your child to learn new words and develop early reading skills. With so many pictures to talk about and familiar objects to match and compare, each page offers a wealth of learning opportunities. Designed to make language fun for the youngest age group, **My First Word Book** opens up a world of discovery and encourages a lasting enjoyment of books.

Betty Root Reading and Language Consultant

Art Editor Penny Britchfield
Editor Sheila Hanly
Production Marguerite Fenn
Managing Editor Jane Yorke
Art Director Roger Priddy

Photography Dave King, Tim Ridley
Illustrations Pat Thorne
Reading Consultant Betty Root

First published in Great Britain in 1991
by Dorling Kindersley Limited,
9 Henrietta Street, London, WC2E 8PS
Reprinted 1991, 1992 (twice), 1993

A CIP catalogue record for this book is
available from the British Library

ISBN 0-86318-630-0
Colour reproduction by J Film Process, Singapore
Printed in Italy by Graphicom

Contents

All about me   4

My clothes   6

At home   8

Around the house   10

In the kitchen   12

Things to eat
and drink   14

In the bathroom   16

In the garden   18

In the toolshed   20

Going out   22

At the park 24

At the supermarket 26

Cars 28

Things that move 30

In the country 32

In the woods 34

On the farm 36

Pets 38

At the zoo 40

Toys 42

Going to school 44

At the seaside 46

Time, weather,
and seasons 48

Sports 50

Action words 52

Playtime words 54

Storybook words 55

Colours, shapes,
and numbers 56

Position words 58

Opposites 60

Index 62

All about me

My face

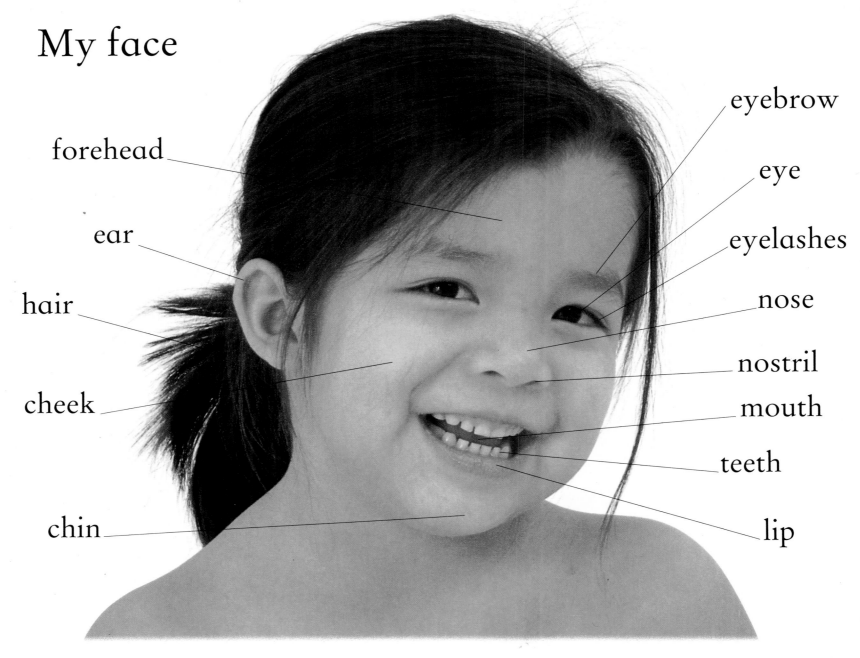

forehead

eyebrow

eye

eyelashes

ear

nose

hair

nostril

mouth

cheek

teeth

chin

lip

My hands

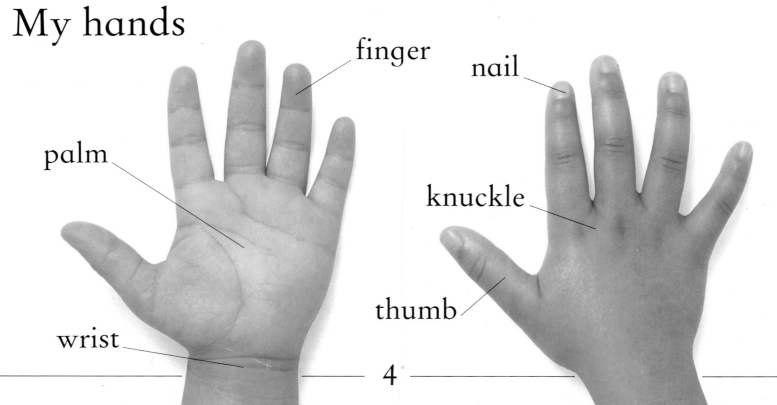

finger

nail

palm

knuckle

thumb

wrist

My body

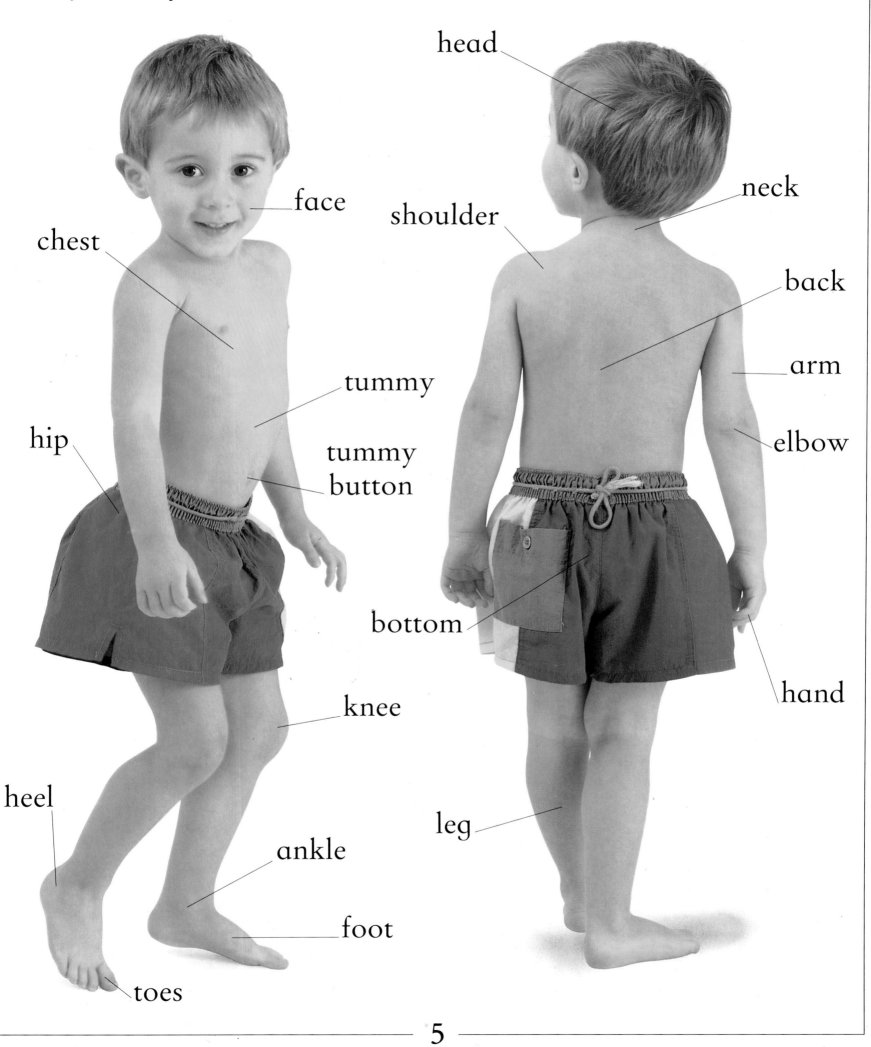

face

chest

hip

heel

tummy

tummy
button

knee

ankle

toes

foot

head

neck

shoulder

back

arm

elbow

bottom

hand

leg

My clothes

buttons

anorak

buckle

belt

cardigan

trousers

braces

jeans

pyjamas

dungarees

straw hat

woolly hat

pants

beads

T-shirt

shorts

watch

socks

slippers

shoes

trainers

sandals

knickers

vest

sweatshirt

hanger

coat

tracksuit

skirt

petticoat

scarf

nightdress

shirt

dress

dressing
gown

4

cap

snowsuit

raincoat

mittens

wellington
boots

gloves

umbrella

jumper

tights

7

At home

attic

cellar

shutters

gutter

drainpipe

ceiling

bed

bedroom

balcony

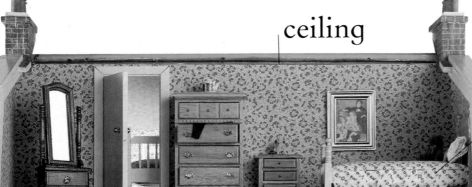

fireplace

sitting room

sofa

bannister

cooker

stairs

carpet

wallpaper

bath   bathroom   kitchen   floor

garage

hedge

drive

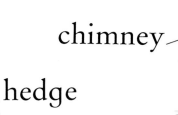

chimney

roof

window

window box

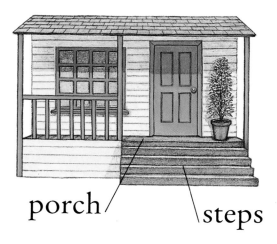

porch

steps

wall

front door

windowsill

A family

grandfather   grandmother   father   mother   daughter   son

Around the house

telephone

hairdryer

sofa

curtains

radiator

picture

vacuum cleaner

radio

record player

book

stool

bookcase

doormat

sewing machine

armchair

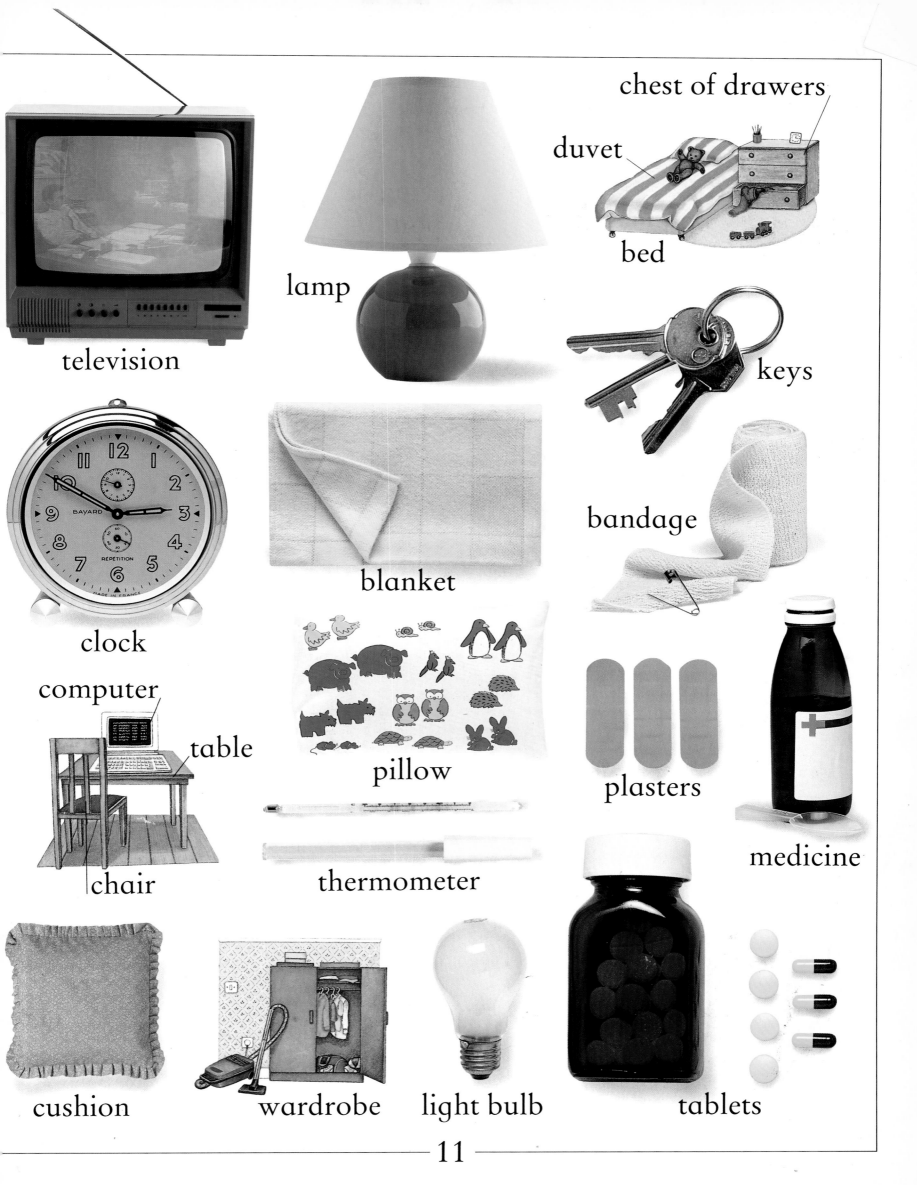

television

lamp

chest of drawers

duvet

bed

keys

clock

blanket

bandage

computer

table

pillow

plasters

medicine

chair

thermometer

cushion

wardrobe

light bulb

tablets

11

In the kitchen

rolling pin

frying pan

rubber gloves

egg cup

brush

dustpan

weighing scales

jug

fridge

food mixer

oven

cooker

plate

place mat

napkin

oven glove

knife

fork

broom

sieve

spoon

apron

kettle

washing machine

mop

glass

bowl

mug

colander

cup

saucer

matches

teapot

cake tin

sink

draining board

saucepan

bin

cupboard

biscuit cutters

ironing board

mixing bowl

high chair

iron

Things to eat and drink

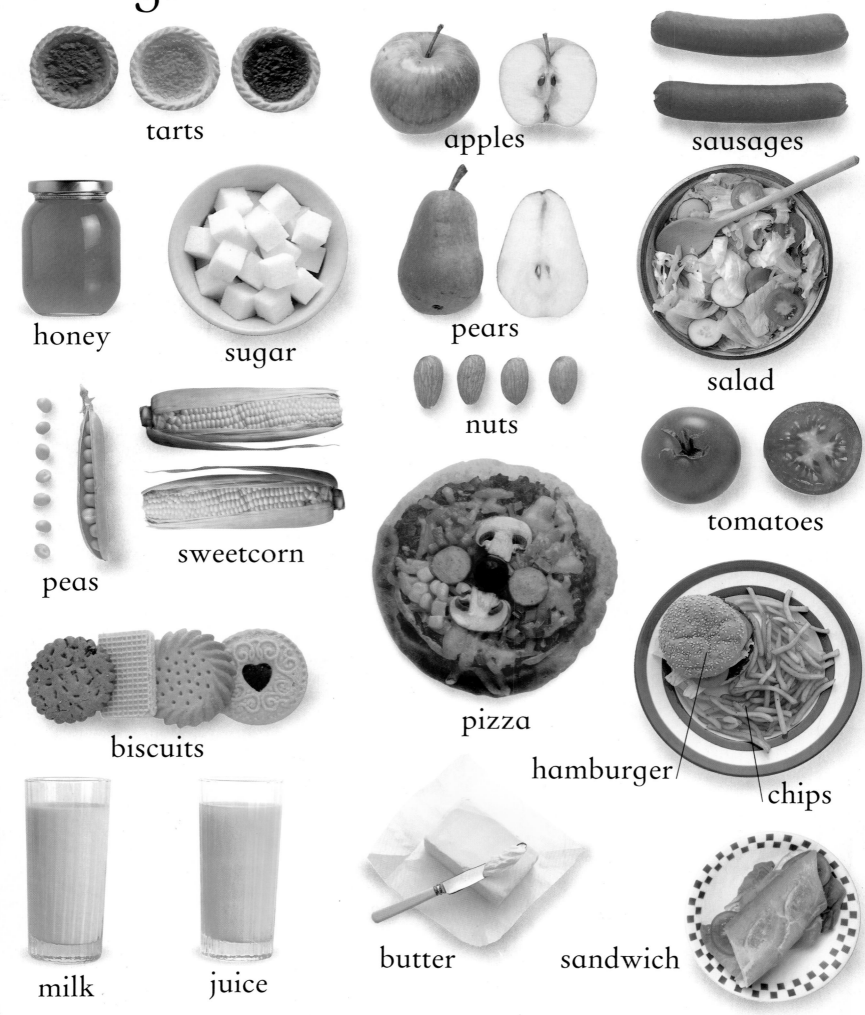

tarts

apples

sausages

honey

sugar

pears

salad

nuts

peas

sweetcorn

pizza

tomatoes

biscuits

hamburger

chips

milk

juice

butter

sandwich

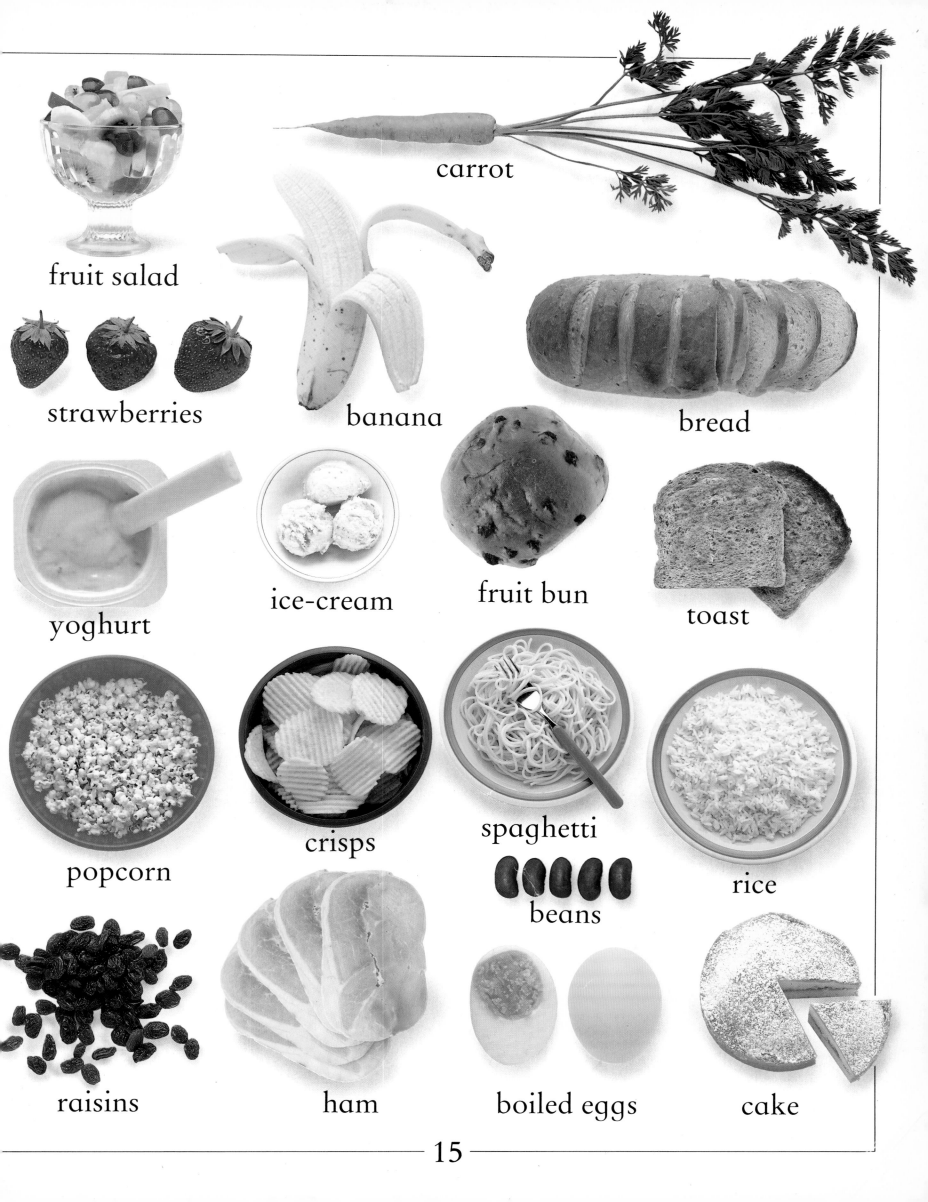

fruit salad

carrot

strawberries

banana

bread

yoghurt

ice-cream

fruit bun

toast

popcorn

crisps

spaghetti

beans

rice

raisins

ham

boiled eggs

cake

In the bathroom

toothpaste

toothbrush

cotton wool
balls

make-up bag

sponges

hairband

tap

towel

washbasin

ribbons

deodorant

hair slide

comb

hairbrush

shampoo

perfume

water

bath

bath mat

talcum powder

potty

16

make-up

tissues

soap

toilet shower

razor

shaving
brush

toy frog

plug

toy duck

nailbrush

mirror

shaving
foam

face flannel

lipstick

bubbles

cotton buds

pot of cream

bubble bath

17

In the garden

trowel

fork

canes

secateurs

flower

petal

stem

lawn

lawn mower

flowerpots

rose

soil

string

wasp

pansies

ladybird

bulbs

sunflower

seedlings

seed tray

daffodils

butterfly

bee

watering can

seeds

spade

rake

pot plant

tulips

weeds

ants

grass

worms

wheelbarrow

greenhouse

snail

hosepipe

nasturtiums

In the toolshed

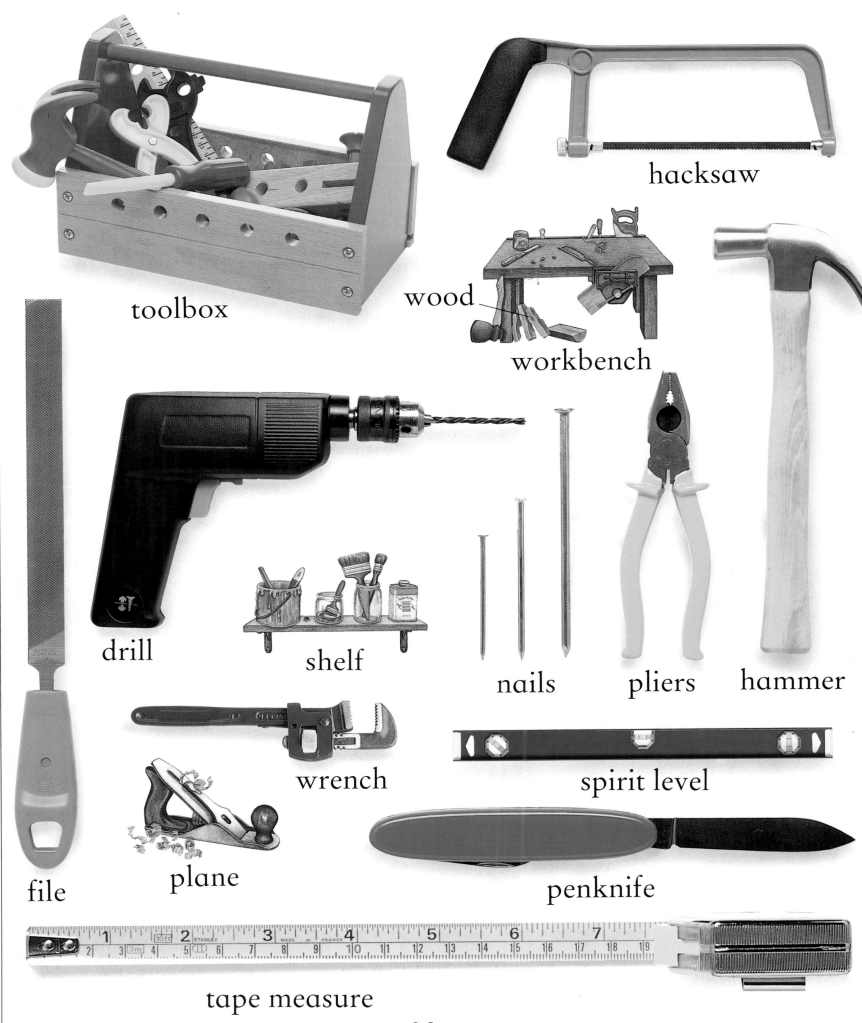

toolbox

hacksaw

wood

workbench

hammer

drill

shelf

nails

pliers

file

wrench

spirit level

plane

penknife

tape measure

20

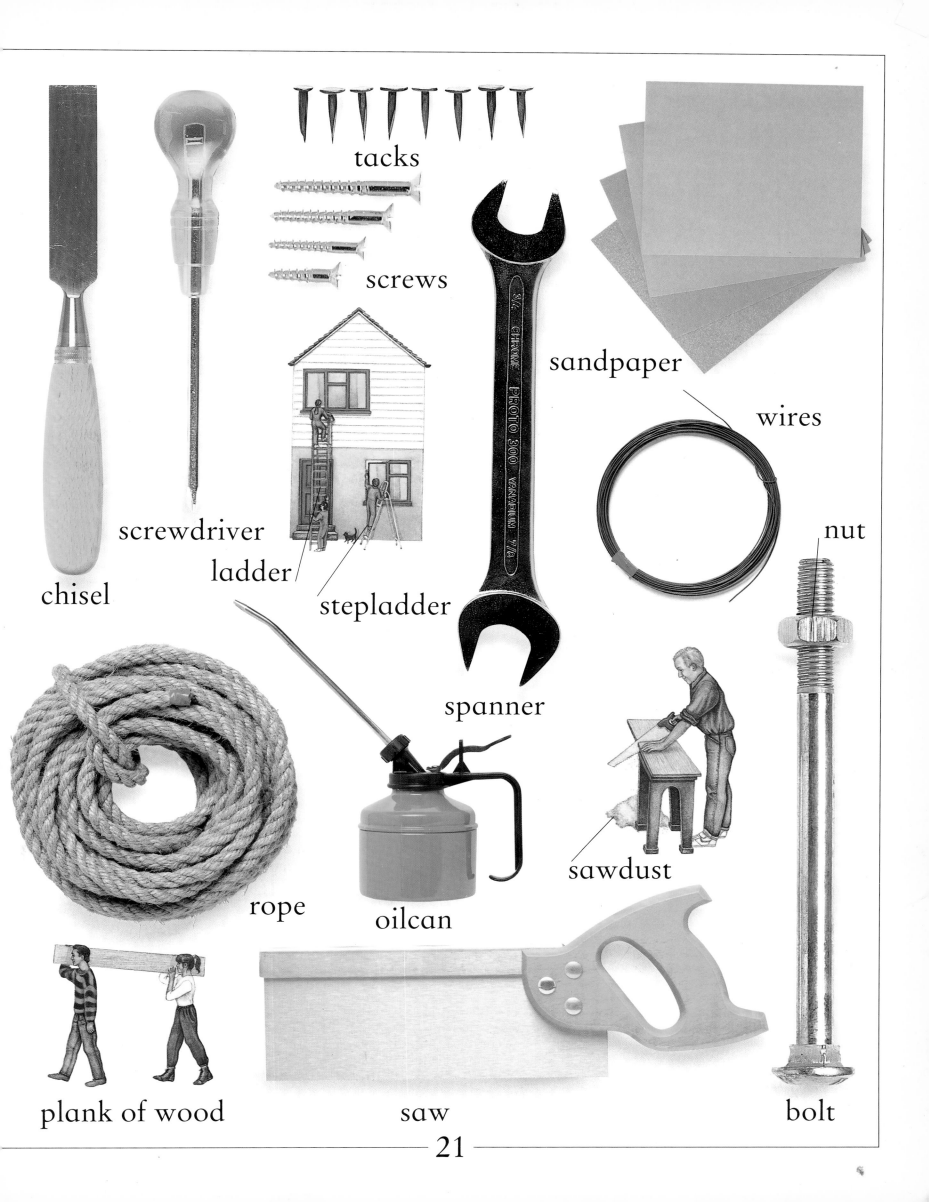

chisel

screwdriver

tacks

screws

ladder

stepladder

sandpaper

wires

spanner

nut

rope

oilcan

sawdust

plank of wood

saw

bolt

Going out

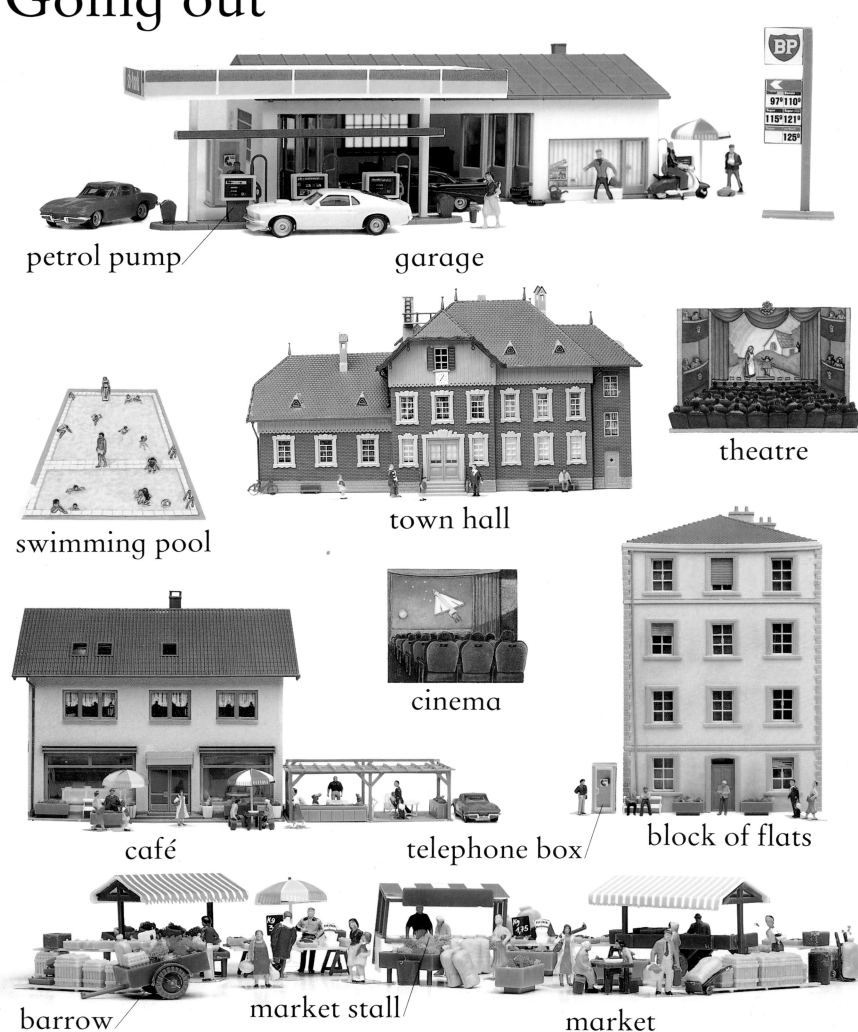

petrol pump

garage

swimming pool

town hall

theatre

cinema

café

telephone box

block of flats

barrow

market stall

market

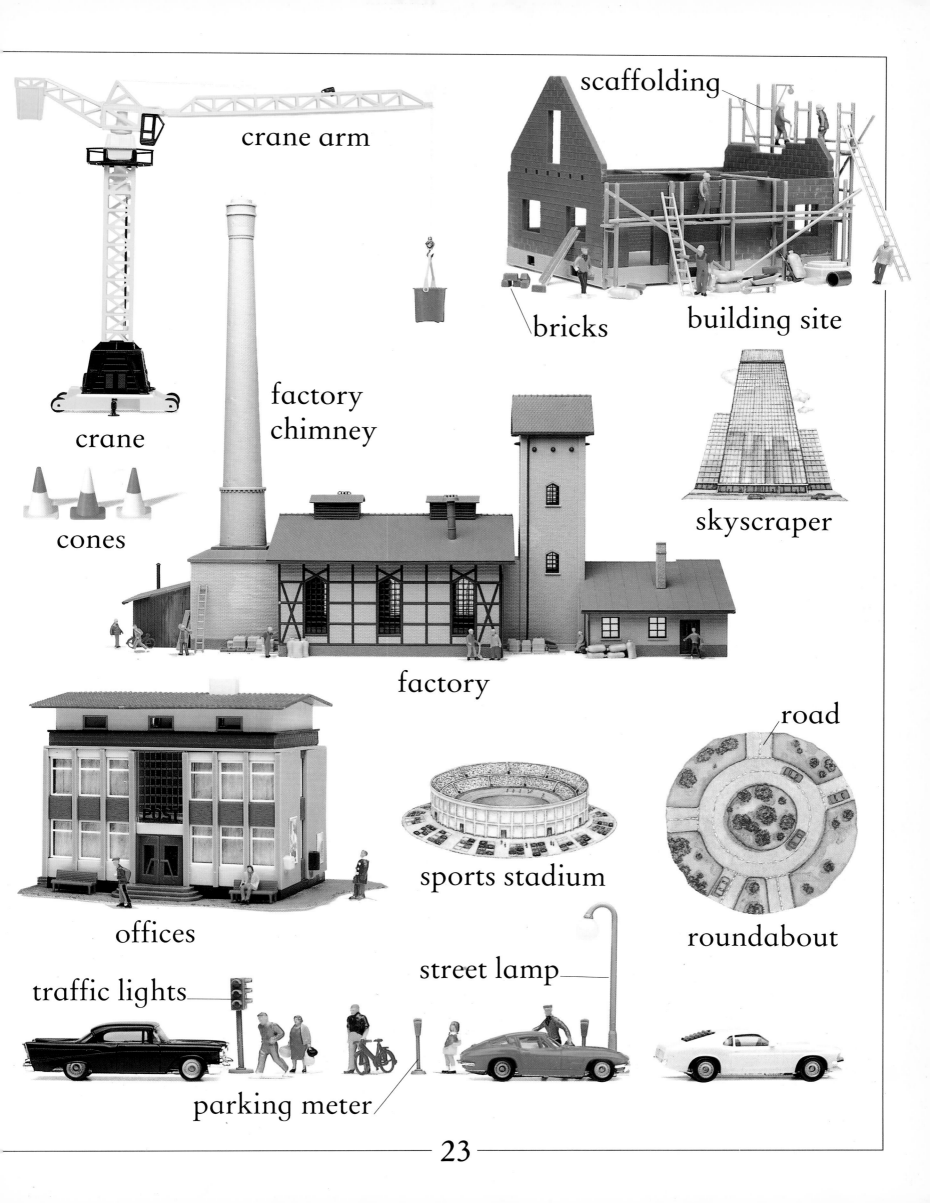

crane arm

scaffolding

bricks

building site

crane

factory chimney

cones

skyscraper

factory

road

offices

sports stadium

roundabout

traffic lights

street lamp

parking meter

23

At the park

picnic basket

picnic

statue

bench

fountain

flowers

buggy

children

tricycle

kite

sandpit

roller skates

roundabout

skipping rope

skateboard

swan

cygnet

climbing frame

swing

slide

seesaw

pigeons

ice-cream van

pram

flask

lunch box

At the supermarket

shopping basket

cereal

vegetable oil

sweets

washing-up liquid

jam

flour

coffee

meat

fish

toilet rolls

Fruit

grapes

peaches

cherries

pineapple

lemon

orange

raspberries

blackcurrants

chocolate

tins

trolley

washing powder

cash register

bottles

cheese

cheque book

purse

box

shop assistant

checkout

money

bag

Vegetables

green beans

celery

pepper

onion

courgettes

cabbage

potatoes

cucumber

lettuce

Cars

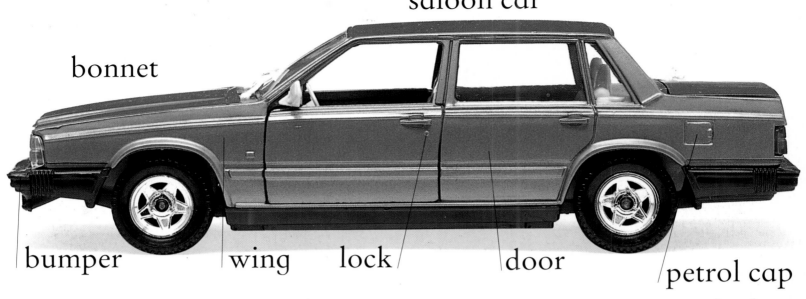

saloon car

bonnet

bumper   wing   lock   door

petrol cap

dashboard

speedometer

indicator

steering wheel

ignition key

engine

NKJ 374T

limousine

tyre

wheel

sports car

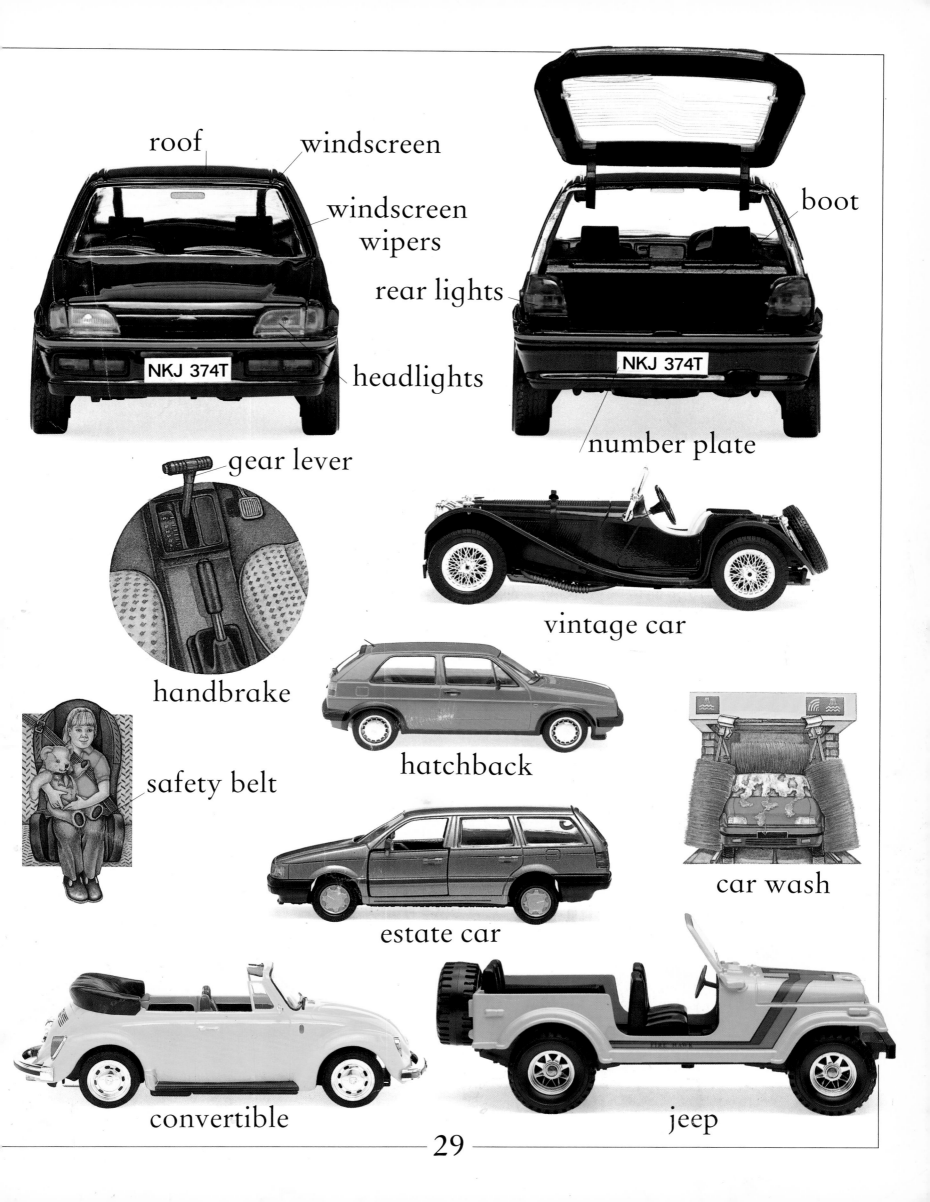

roof

windscreen

windscreen wipers

boot

rear lights

headlights

NKJ 374T

NKJ 374T

number plate

gear lever

handbrake

vintage car

safety belt

hatchback

car wash

estate car

convertible

jeep

29

Things that move

bicycle

digger

scooter

car

car ferry

taxi

lorry

boat

bulldozer

airship

submarine

carriage

parachutes

motorbike

railway
line

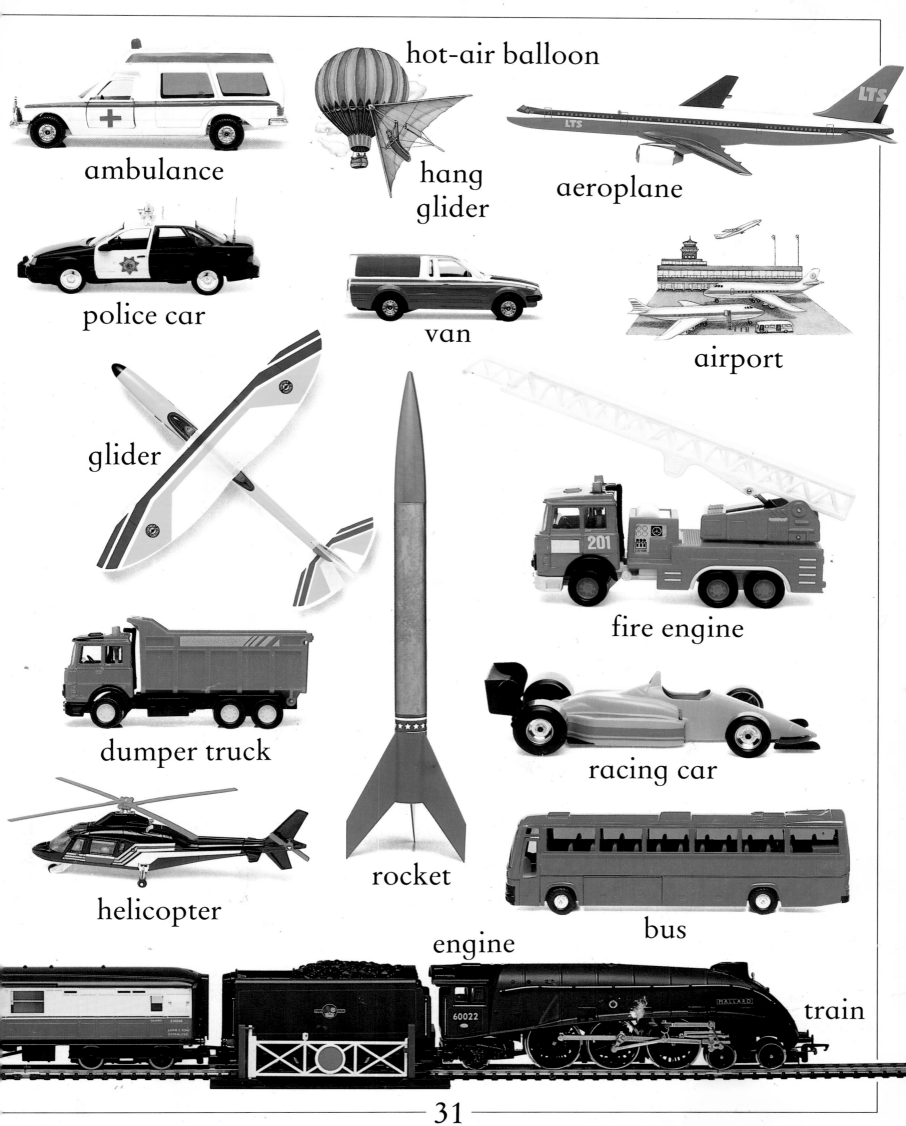

ambulance

hot-air balloon

hang glider

aeroplane

police car

van

airport

glider

fire engine

dumper truck

rocket

racing car

helicopter

engine

bus

train

In the country

orchard

village

rabbit

dragonfly

waterlilies

stream

mountain

valley

lake

island

hills

bridge

river

ferns

toad

mushrooms

road

blackberries

fox

caravan

tent

campsite

Wild flowers

waterfall

dandelion

buttercups

daisies

In the woods

tree

acorns

plums

pine cones

blossom

berries

fir needles

twig

squirrel

bird's eggs

bird

chick

branch

bird's nest

owl

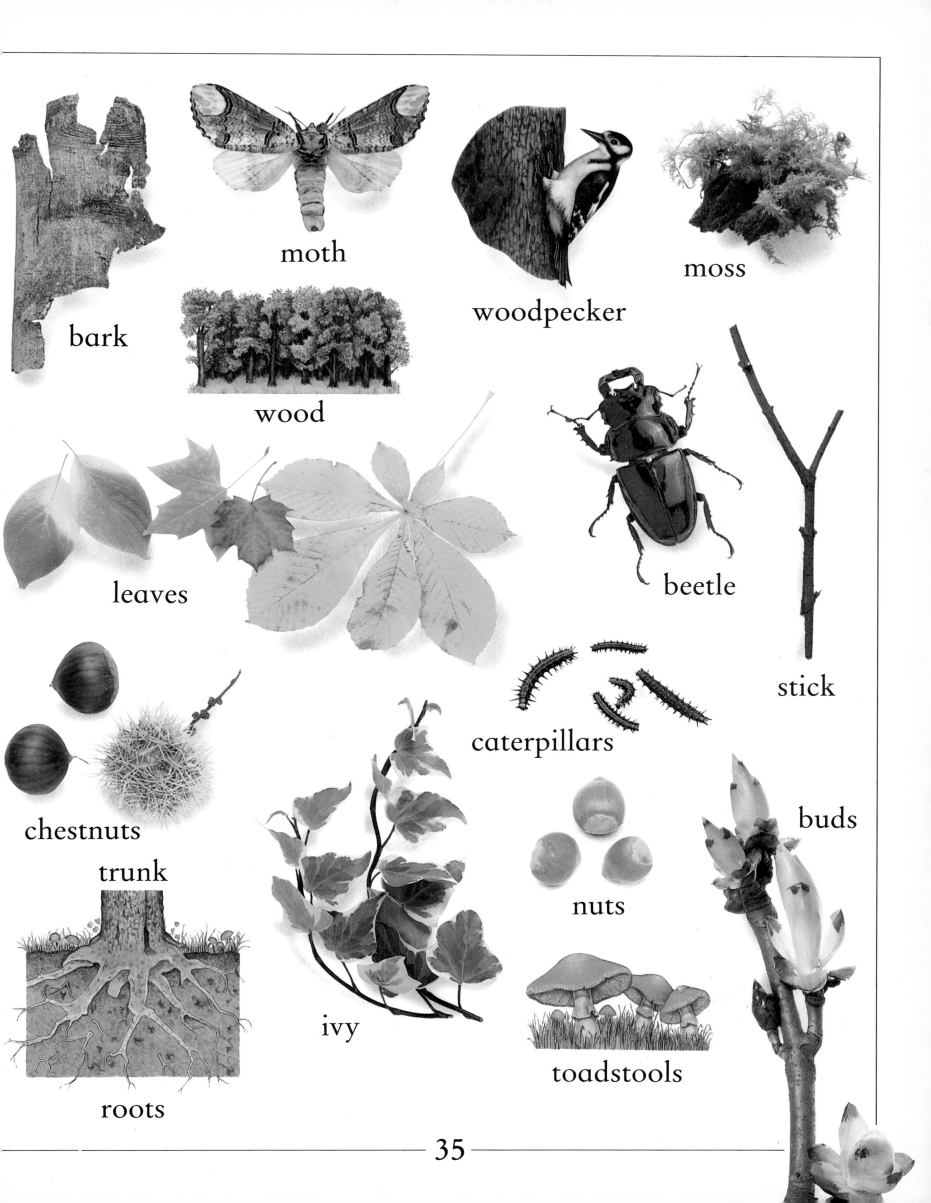

bark

moth

woodpecker

moss

wood

leaves

beetle

stick

chestnuts

caterpillars

buds

trunk

ivy

nuts

toadstools

roots

35

On the farm

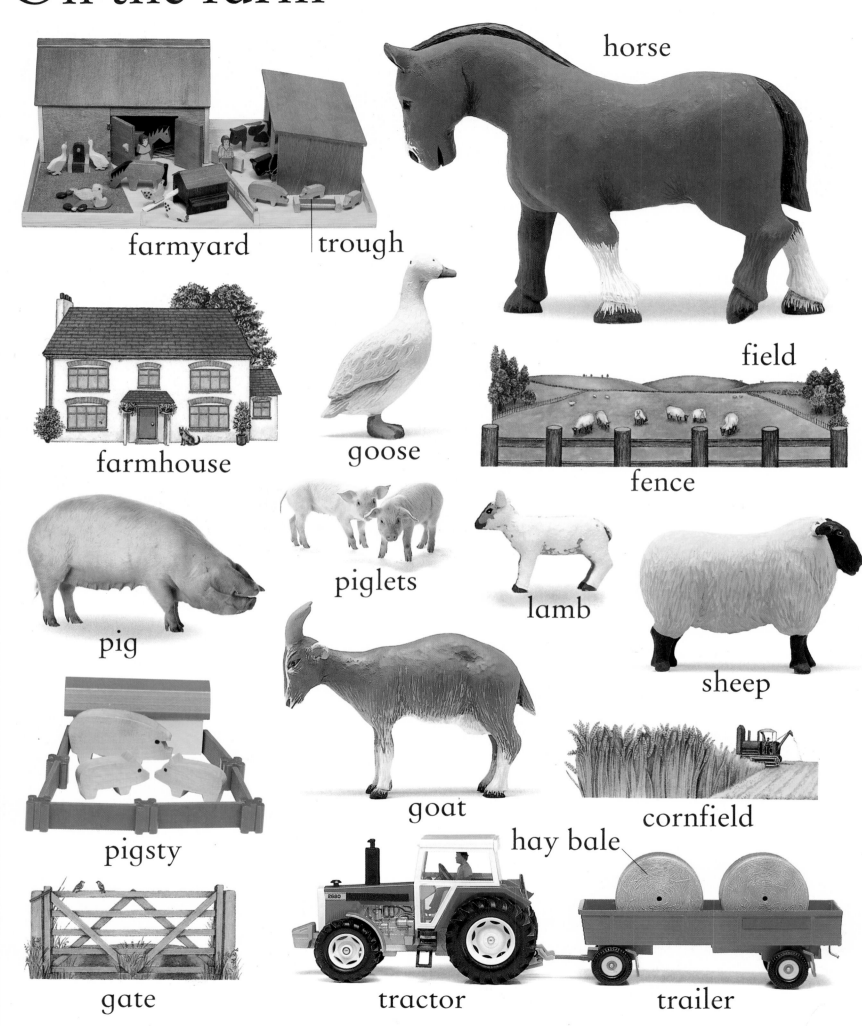

farmyard

trough

horse

farmhouse

goose

field

fence

pig

piglets

lamb

sheep

pigsty

goat

cornfield

hay bale

gate

tractor

trailer

bull

calf

cow

hen coop

chick

stable

hen

pond

cockerel

sheepdog

ducklings

duck

barn

plough

combine harvester

Pets

hamsters

shell

tortoise

whiskers

parrots

beak

tadpoles

tail

cat

feathers

guinea pig

water weed

goldfish

fish tank

puppies

collar

lead

bone

fur

mouse

dog

paw

perch

canary

cage

kittens

basket

mane

pony

hoof

wing

claws

budgerigar

39

At the zoo

crocodile

scales

pelican

leopard

peacock

kangaroo

horns

fin

dolphin

gazelle

hippopotamus

shark

tiger

chimpanzee

ostrich

giraffe

bear

40

lizard

rhinoceros

penguin

camel

panda

polar bear

bison

koala

tusk

trunk

elephant

lion

snake

zebra

anteater

Toys

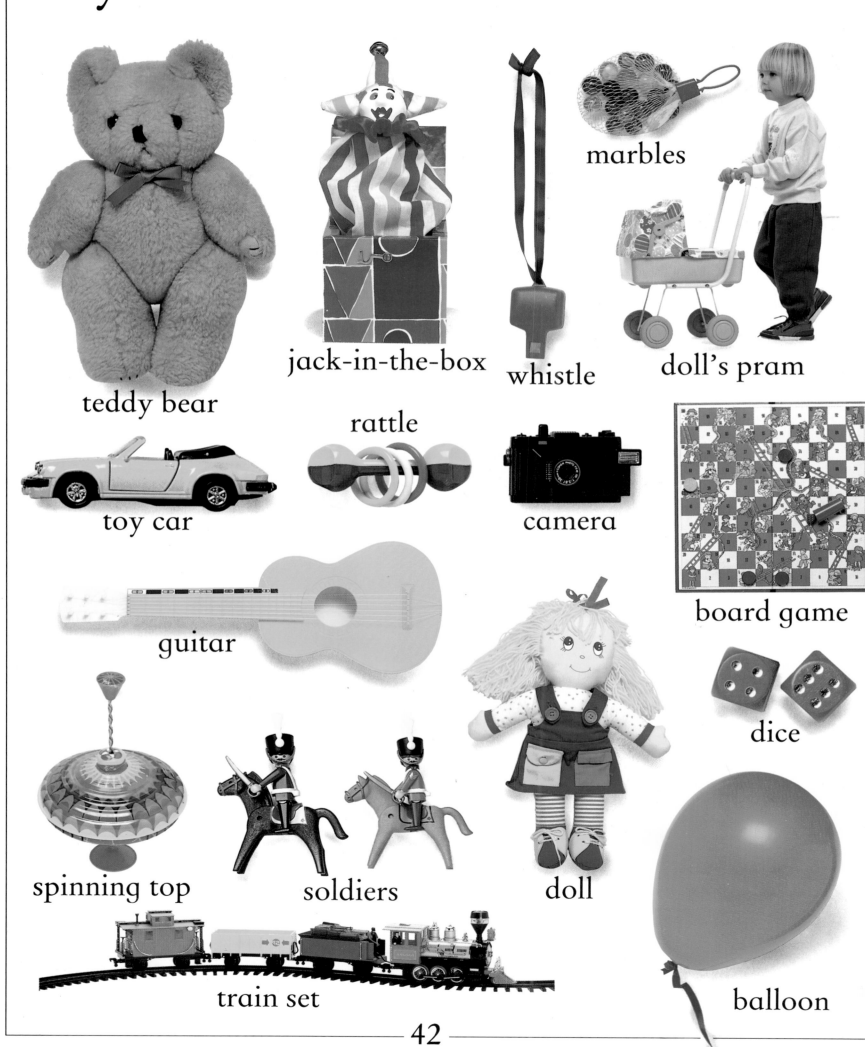

teddy bear

jack-in-the-box

whistle

marbles

doll's pram

rattle

toy car

camera

board game

guitar

dice

spinning top

soldiers

doll

train set

balloon

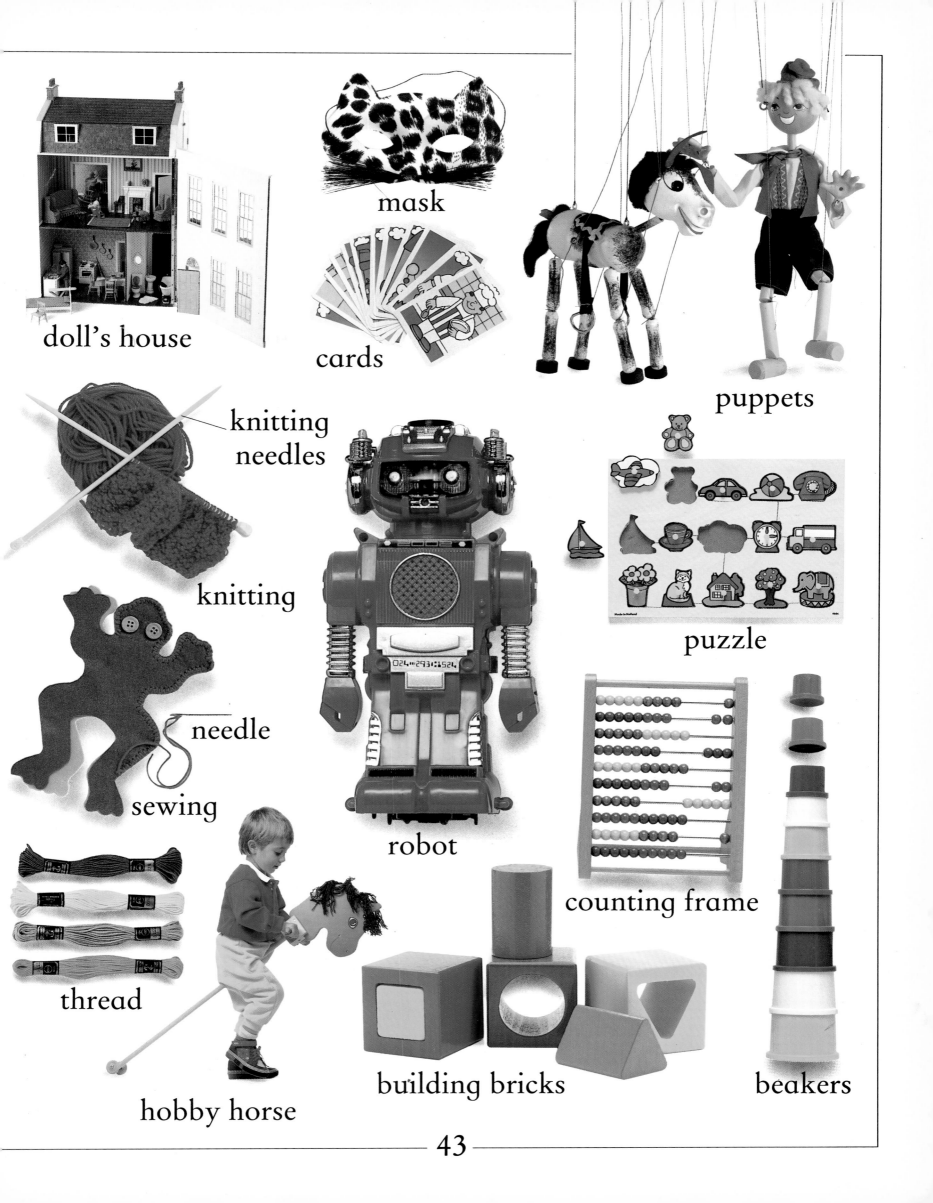

doll's house

mask

cards

puppets

knitting needles

knitting

needle

sewing

robot

puzzle

counting frame

thread

hobby horse

building bricks

beakers

43

Going to school

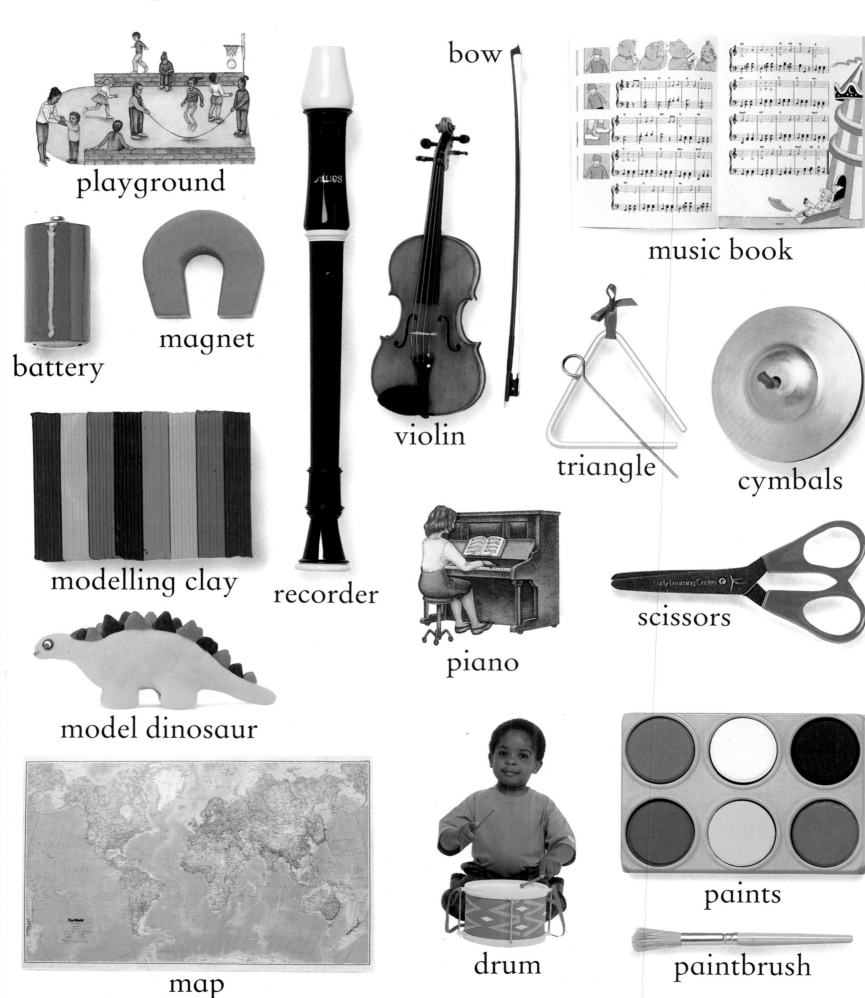

playground

battery

magnet

modelling clay

model dinosaur

map

bow

recorder

violin

piano

drum

music book

triangle

cymbals

scissors

paints

paintbrush

abcdefg
hijklm
nopqrst
uvwxyz

letters

teacher

writing

books

globe

glue

chalk

blackboard

1 2 3 4 5 6 7 8 9 10
numbers

pencil

calendar

rubber

paper

drawing

painting

ruler

crayons

easel

At the seaside

flag

sandcastle

pebbles

rocks

deckchair

toy windmill

rubber ring

cliffs

sea

beach

waves

fish

sand

harbour

starfish

shell

seaweed

armbands

sunglasses

ice-cream cone

lighthouse

beach umbrella

seagulls

crab

swimsuit

beach ball

spade

handle

sun hat

sail

bucket

rock pool

sailing boat

47

Time, weather, and seasons

Time

daytime

breakfast-time

playtime

bedtime

lunchtime

dinnertime

night-time

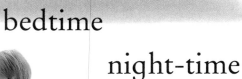

Days of the week

Sunday	Thursday
Monday	Friday
Tuesday	Saturday
Wednesday	

Months of the year

January	May	September
February	June	October
March	July	November
April	August	December

Weather

sun

cloud

rainbow

rain

puddle

wind

snowman

snow

Seasons

spring

summer

autumn

winter

Sports

helmet

American
football

skating

ice skate

American football

shuttlecocks

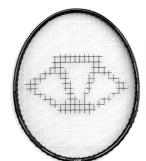

boxing gloves

darts

skiing

skis

badminton
racquet

fishing net

horse
riding

fishing rod

basketball

tennis

net

football

tennis racquet

table-tennis bat

cycling

football

cricket bat

baseball bat

skittles

mask

snorkel

baseball

yacht

golf club

hockey stick

Slazenger

51

Action words

reading

counting

eating

drinking

picking up

hugging

crying

sweeping

giving   taking

pushing

pulling

looking

whispering

shouting

listening

talking

pointing

standing

sitting

laughing

smiling

kissing

sleeping

running

walking

carrying

lying down

crawling

Playtime words

skipping

kicking

hitting

playing

climbing

building

dancing

chasing

hopping

falling over

jumping

blowing   throwing   catching

hiding

riding

Storybook words

Indian chief

dragon

armour

knight

reindeer

sledge

Father Christmas

pirate

crown

cloak

dinosaur

cowboy

fairy

monster

king

queen

sword

wand

castle

witch

giant

prince

princess

wizard

beanstalk

broomstick

pumpkin

Colours, shapes, and numbers

Colours

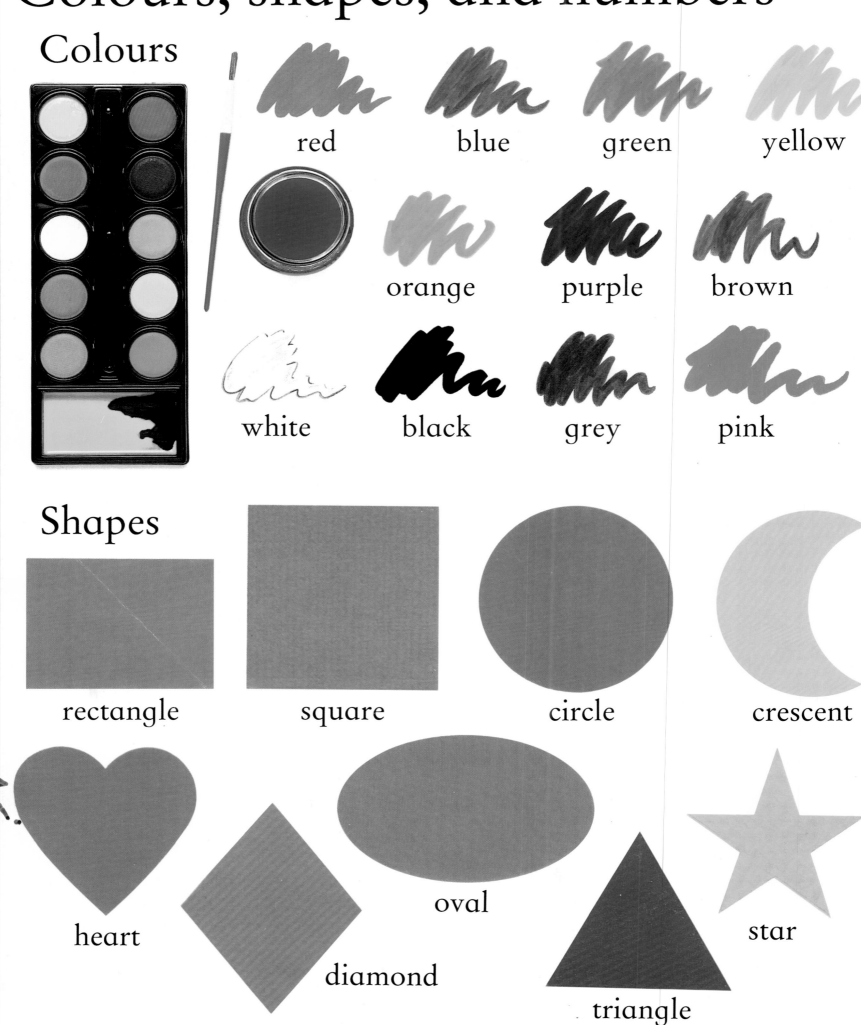

red

blue

green

yellow

orange

purple

brown

white

black

grey

pink

Shapes

rectangle

square

circle

crescent

heart

diamond

oval

triangle

star

Numbers

1	2	3	4	5	6	7
one	two	three	four	five	six	seven

8	9	10	11	12
eight	nine	ten	eleven	twelve

13	14	15	16
thirteen	fourteen	fifteen	sixteen

17	18	19	20
seventeen	eighteen	nineteen	twenty

Position words

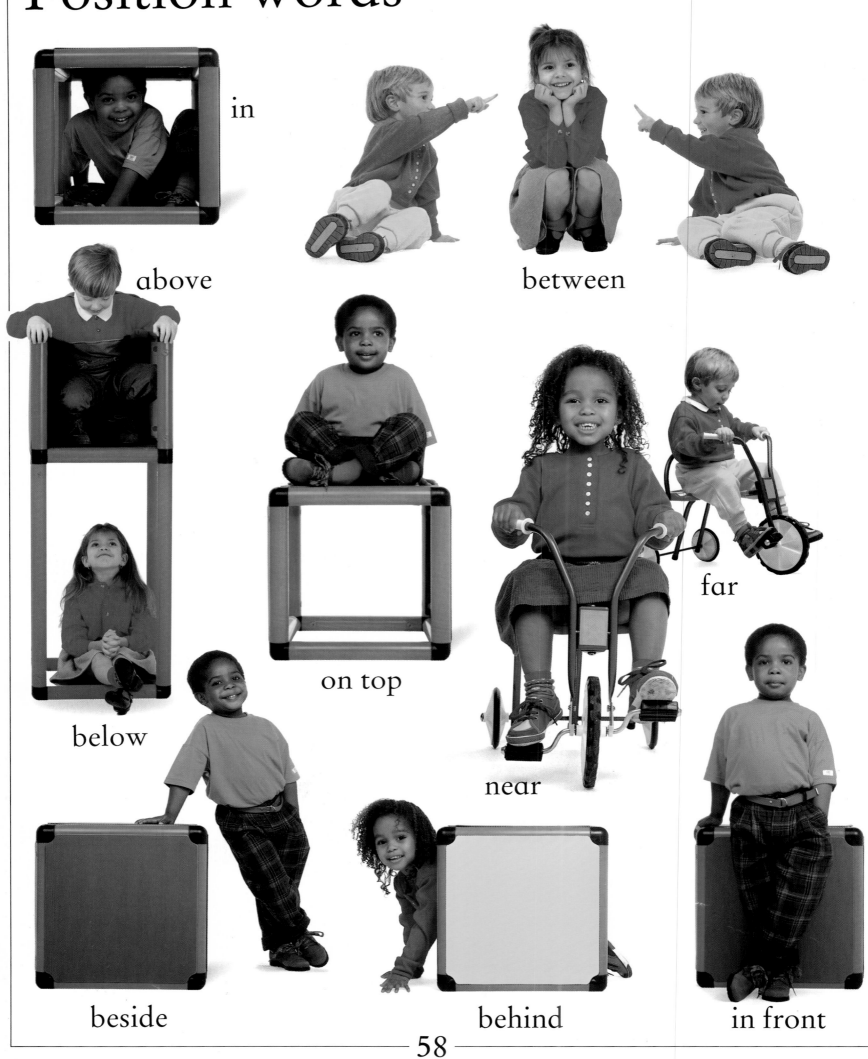

in

above

between

below

on top

far

near

beside

behind

in front

58

up

down

top

on

off

over

under

bottom

last

third

second

first

59

Opposites

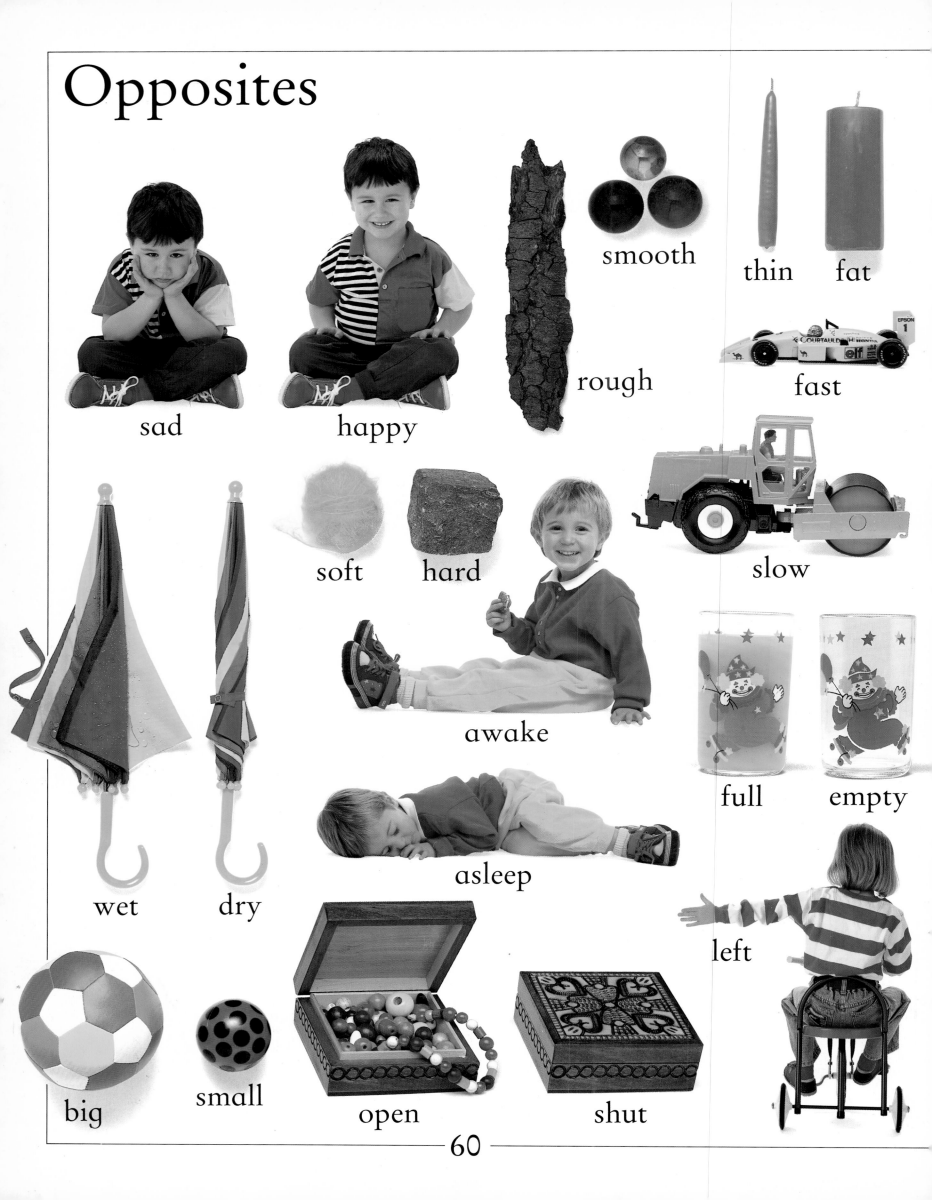

smooth

thin   fat

rough

fast

sad   happy

soft   hard

slow

awake

full   empty

wet   dry

asleep

left

big   small   open   shut

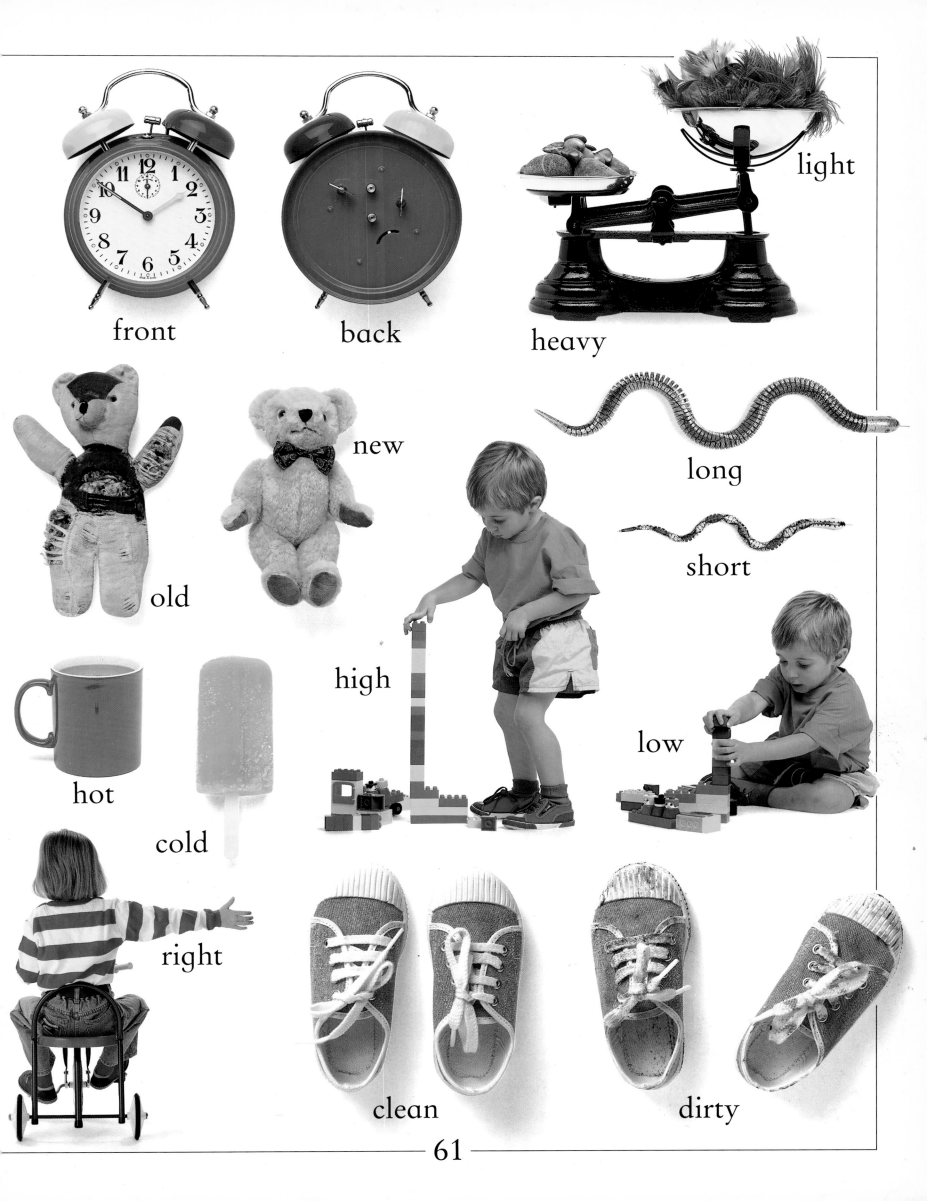

front

back

light

heavy

new

old

long

short

high

hot

cold

low

right

clean

dirty

61

Index

Above ...58
acorns ...34
aeroplane ...31
airport ...31
airship ...30
ambulance ...31
American football ...50
ankle ...5
anorak ...6
anteater ...41
ants ...19
apples ...14
April ...48
apron ...12
arm ...5
armbands ...47
armchair ...10
armour ...55
asleep ...60
attic ...8
August ...48
autumn ...49
awake ...60

Back ...5, 61
badminton racquet ...50
bag ...27
balcony ...8
balloon ...42
banana ...15
bandage ...11
bannister ...8
bark ...35
barn ...37
barrow ...22
baseball ...51
baseball bat ...51
basket ...39
basketball ...51
bath ...8, 16
bath mat ...16
bathroom ...8
battery ...44
beach ...46
beach ball ...47
beach umbrella ...47
beads ...6
beak ...38
beakers ...43
beans ...15
beanstalk ...55
bear ...40
bed ...8, 11
bedroom ...8
bedtime ...48
bee ...19
beetle ...35
behind ...58
below ...58
belt ...6
bench ...24
berries ...34
beside ...58
between ...58
bicycle ...30
big ...60
bin ...13

bird ...34
bird's eggs ...34
bird's nest ...34
biscuit cutters ...13
biscuits ...14
bison ...41
black ...56
blackberries ...33
blackboard ...45
blackcurrants ...26
blanket ...11
block of flats ...22
blossom ...34
blowing ...54
blue ...56
board game ...42
boat ...30
body ...5
boiled eggs ...15
bolt ...21
bone ...39
bonnet ...28
book ...10
books ...45
bookcase ...10
boot ...29
bottles ...27
bottom ...5, 59
bow ...44
bowl ...13
box ...27
boxing gloves ...50
braces ...6
branch ...34
bread ...15
breakfast-time ...48
bricks ...23
bridge ...32
broom ...12
broomstick ...55
brown ...56
brush ...12
bubble bath ...17
bubbles ...17
bucket ...47
buckle ...6
budgerigar ...39
buds ...35
buggy ...24
building ...54
building bricks ...43
building site ...23
bulbs ...18
bull ...37
bulldozer ...30
bumper ...28
bus ...31
butter ...14
buttercups ...33
butterfly ...19
buttons ...6

Cabbage ...27
café ...22
cage ...39
cake ...15
cake tin ...13
calendar ...45

calf ...37
camel ...41
camera ...42
campsite ...33
canary ...39
canes ...18
cap ...7
car ...30
car ferry ...30
car wash ...29
caravan ...33
cardigan ...6
cards ...43
carpet ...8
carriage ...30
carrot ...15
carrying ...53
cash register ...27
castle ...55
cat ...38
catching ...54
caterpillars ...35
ceiling ...8
celery ...27
cellar ...8
cereal ...26
chair ...11
chalk ...45
chasing ...54
checkout ...27
cheek ...4
cheese ...27
cheque book ...27
cherries ...26
chest ...5
chest of drawers ...11
chestnuts ...35
chick ...34, 37
children ...24
chimney ...9
chimpanzee ...40
chin ...4
chips ...14
chisel ...21
chocolate ...27
cinema ...22
circle ...56
claws ...39
clean ...61
cliffs ...46
climbing ...54
climbing frame ...25
cloak ...55
clock ...11
cloud ...49
coat ...7
cockerel ...37
coffee ...26
colander ...13
cold ...61
collar ...39
colours ...56
comb ...16
combine harvester ...37
computer ...11
cones ...23
convertible ...29

cooker ...8, 12
cornfield ...36
cotton buds ...17
cotton wool balls ...16
counting ...52
counting frame ...43
courgettes ...27
cow ...37
cowboy ...55
crab ...47
crane ...23
crane arm ...23
crawling ...53
crayons ...45
crescent ...56
cricket bat ...51
crisps ...15
crocodile ...40
crown ...55
crying ...52
cucumber ...27
cup ...13
cupboard ...13
curtains ...10
cushion ...11
cycling ...50
cygnet ...25
cymbals ...44

Daffodils ...19
daisies ...33
dancing ...54
dandelion ...33
darts ...50
dashboard ...28
daughter ...9
days ...48
daytime ...48
December ...48
deckchair ...46
deodorant ...16
diamond ...56
dice ...42
digger ...30
dinnertime ...48
dinosaur ...55
dirty ...61
dog ...39
doll ...42
doll's house ...43
doll's pram ...42
dolphin ...40
door ...28
doormat ...10
down ...59
dragon ...55
dragonfly ...32
draining board ...13
drainpipe ...8
drawing ...45
dress ...7
dressing gown ...7
drill ...20
drinking ...52
drive ...9
drum ...44
dry ...60
duck ...37

ducklings ...37
dumper truck ...31
dungarees ...6
dustpan ...12
duvet ...11

Ear ...4
easel ...45
eating ...52
egg cup ...12
eight ...57
eighteen ...57
elbow ...5
elephant ...41
eleven ...57
empty ...60
engine ...28, 31
estate car ...29
eye ...4
eyebrow ...4
eyelashes ...4

Face ...5
face flannel ...17
factory ...23
factory chimney ...23
fairy ...55
falling over ...54
family ...9
far ...58
farmhouse ...36
farmyard ...36
fast ...60
fat ...60
father ...9
Father Christmas ...55
feathers ...38
February ...48
fence ...36
ferns ...32
field ...36
fifteen ...57
file ...20
fin ...40
finger ...4
fir needles ...34
fire engine ...31
fireplace ...8
first ...59
fish ...26, 46
fish tank ...38
fishing net ...50
fishing rod ...50
five ...57
flag ...46
flask ...25
floor ...8
flour ...26
flower ...18, 24
flowerpots ...18
food mixer ...12
foot ...5
football ...50
forehead ...4
fork ...12, 18
fountain ...24
four ...57
fourteen ...57

fox ...33
Friday ...48
fridge ...12
front ...61
front door ...9
fruit ...26
fruit bun ...15
fruit salad ...15
frying pan ...12
full ...60
fur ...39

Garage ...9, 22
gate ...36
gazelle ...40
gear lever ...29
giant ...55
giraffe ...40
giving ...52
glass ...13
glider ...31
globe ...45
gloves ...7
glue ...45
goat ...36
goldfish ...38
golf club ...51
goose ...36
grandfather ...9
grandmother ...9
grapes ...26
grass ...19
green ...56
green beans ...27
greenhouse ...19
grey ...56
guinea pig ...38
guitar ...42
gutter ...8

Hacksaw ...20
hair ...4
hair slide ...16
hairband ...16
hairbrush ...16
hairdryer ...10
ham ...15
hamburger ...14
hammer ...20
hamsters ...38
hand ...5
handbrake ...29
handle ...47
hang glider ...31
hanger ...7
happy ...60
harbour ...46
hard ...60
hatchback ...29
hay bale ...36
head ...5
headlights ...29
heart ...56
heavy ...61
hedge ...9
heel ...5
helicopter ...31
helmet ...50
hen ...37
hen coop ...37
hiding ...54

high ...61
high chair ...13
hills ...32
hip ...5
hippopotamus ...40
hitting ...54
hobby horse ...43
hockey stick ...50
honey ...14
hoof ...39
hopping ...54
horns ...40
horse ...36
horse riding ...50
hosepipe ...19
hot ...61
hot-air balloon ...31
hugging ...52

Ice-cream ...15
ice-cream cone ...47
ice-cream van ...25
ice skate ...50
ignition key ...28
in ...58
in front ...58
Indian chief ...55
indicator ...28
iron ...13
ironing board ...13
island ...32
ivy ...35

Jack-in-the-box ...42
jam ...26
January ...48
jeans ...6
jeep ...29
jug ...12
juice ...14
July ...48
jumper ...7
jumping ...54
June ...48

Kangaroo ...40
kettle ...13
keys ...11
kicking ...54
king ...55
kissing ...53
kitchen ...8
kite ...24
kittens ...39
knee ...5
knickers ...6
knife ...12
knight ...55
knitting ...43
knitting needles ...43
knuckle ...4
koala ...41

Ladder ...21
ladybirds ...18
lake ...32
lamb ...36
lamp ...11
last ...59
laughing ...53
lawn ...18
lawn mower ...18

lead ...39
leaves ...35
left ...60
leg ...5
lemon ...26
leopard ...40
letters ...45
lettuce ...27
light ...61
light bulb ...11
lighthouse ...47
limousine ...28
lion ...41
lip ...4
lipstick ...17
listening ...53
lizard ...41
lock ...28
long ...61
looking ...52
lorry ...30
low ...61
lunch box ...25
lunchtime ...48
lying down ...53

Magnet ...44
make-up ...17
make-up bag ...16
mane ...39
map ...44
marbles ...42
March ...48
market ...22
market stall ...22
mask ...43, 51
matches ...13
May ...48
meat ...26
medicine ...11
milk ...14
mirror ...17
mittens ...7
mixing bowl ...13
model dinosaur ...44
modelling clay ...44
Monday ...48
money ...27
monster ...55
months ...48
mop ...13
moss ...35
moth ...35
mother ...9
motorbike ...30
mountain ...32
mouse ...39
mouth ...4
mug ...13
mushrooms ...33
music book ...44

Nail ...4
nailbrush ...17
nails ...20
napkin ...12
nasturtiums ...19
near ...58
neck ...5
needle ...43
net ...51

new ...61
night-time ...48
nightdress ...7
nine ...57
nineteen ...57
nose ...4
nostril ...4
November ...48
numbers ...45, 57
nut ...21
nuts ...14, 35

October ...48
off ...59
offices ...23
oilcan ...21
old ...61
on ...59
on top ...58
one ...57
onion ...27
open ...60
orange ...26, 56
orchard ...32
ostrich ...40
oval ...56
oven ...12
oven glove ...12
over ...59
owl ...34

Paintbrush ...44
painting ...45
paints ...44
palm ...4
panda ...41
pansies ...18
pants ...6
paper ...45
parachutes ...30
parking meter ...23
parrots ...38
paw ...39
peaches ...26
peacock ...40
pears ...14
peas ...14
pebbles ...46
pelican ...40
pencil ...45
penguin ...41
penknife ...20
pepper ...27
perch ...39
perfume ...16
petal ...18
petrol cap ...28
petrol pump ...22
petticoat ...7
piano ...44
picking up ...52
picnic ...24
picnic basket ...24
picture ...10
pig ...36
pigeons ...25
piglets ...36
pigsty ...36
pillow ...11
pineapple ...26
pine cones ...34

pink ...56
pirate ...55
pizza ...14
place mat ...12
plane ...20
plank of wood ...21
plasters ...11
plate ...12
playground ...44
playing ...54
playtime ...48
pliers ...20
plough ...37
plug ...17
plums ...34
pointing ...53
polar bear ...41
police car ...31
pond ...37
pony ...39
popcorn ...15
porch ...9
potatoes ...27
pot of cream ...17
pot plant ...19
potty ...16
pram ...25
prince ...55
princess ...55
puddle ...49
pulling ...52
pumpkin ...55
puppets ...43
puppies ...38
purple ...56
purse ...27
pushing ...52
puzzle ...43
pyjamas ...6

Queen ...55

Rabbit ...32
racing car ...31
radiator ...10
radio ...10
railway line ...30
rain ...49
rainbow ...49
raincoat ...7
raisins ...15
rake ...19
raspberries ...26
rattle ...42
razor ...17
reading ...52
rear lights ...29
record player ...10
recorder ...44
rectangle ...56
red ...56
reindeer ...55
rhinoceros ...41
ribbons ...16
rice ...15
riding ...54
right ...61
river ...32
road ...23, 33
robot ...43
rock pool ...47

rocket ...31
rocks ...46
roller skates ...24
rolling pin ...12
roof ...9, 29
roots ...35
rope ...21
rose ...18
rough ...60
roundabout ...23, 24
rubber ...45
rubber gloves ...12
rubber ring ...46
ruler ...45
running ...53

Sad ...60
safety belt ...29
sail ...47
sailing boat ...47
salad ...14
saloon car ...28
sand ...46
sandals ...6
sandcastle ...46
sandpaper ...21
sandpit ...24
sandwich ...14
Saturday ...48
saucepan ...13
saucer ...13
sausages ...14
saw ...21
sawdust ...21
scaffolding ...23
scales ...40
scarf ...7
scissors ...44
scooter ...30
screwdriver ...21
screws ...21
sea ...46
seagulls ...47
seasons ...49
seaweed ...46
secateurs ...18
second ...59
seed tray ...19
seedlings ...19
seeds ...19
seesaw ...25
September ...48
seven ...57
seventeen ...57
sewing ...43
sewing machine ...10
shampoo ...16
shapes ...56
shark ...40
shaving brush ...17
shaving foam ...17
sheep ...36
sheepdog ...37
shelf ...20
shell ...38, 46
shirt ...7
shoes ...6
shop assistant ...27
shopping basket ...26
short ...61
shorts ...6

shoulder ...5
shouting ...53
shower ...17
shut ...60
shutters ...8
shuttlecocks ...50
sieve ...12
sink ...13
sitting ...53
sitting room ...8
six ...57
sixteen ...57
skateboard ...25
skating ...50
skiing ...50
skipping ...54
skipping rope ...25
skirt ...7
skis ...50
skittles ...51
skyscraper ...23
sledge ...55
sleeping ...53
slide ...25
slippers ...6
slow ...60
small ...60
smiling ...53
smooth ...60
snail ...19
snake ...41
snorkel ...51
snow ...49
snowman ...49
snowsuit ...7
soap ...17
socks ...6
sofa ...8, 10
soft ...60
soil ...18
soldiers ...42
son ...9
spade ...19, 47
spaghetti ...15
spanner ...21
speedometer ...28
spinning top ...42
spirit level ...20
sponges ...16
spoon ...12
sports car ...28
sports stadium ...23
spring ...49
square ...56
squirrel ...34
stable ...37
stairs ...8
standing ...53
star ...56
starfish ...46
statue ...24
steering wheel ...28
stem ...18
stepladder ...21
steps ...9
stick ...35
stool ...10
straw hat ...6
strawberries ...15
stream ...32
street lamp ...23

string ...18
submarine ...30
sugar ...14
summer ...49
sun ...49
sun hat ...47
Sunday ...48
sunflower ...18
sunglasses ...47
swan ...25
sweatshirt ...7
sweeping ...52
sweetcorn ...14
sweets ...26
swimming pool ...22
swimsuit ...47
swing ...25
sword ...55

T-shirt ...6
table ...11
table-tennis bat ...51
tablets ...11
tacks ...21
tadpoles ...38
tail ...38
taking ...52
talcum powder ...16
talking ...53
tape measure ...20
tap ...16
tarts ...14
taxi ...30
teacher ...45
teapot ...13
teddy bear ...42
teeth ...4
telephone ...10
telephone box ...22
television ...11
ten ...57
tennis ...51
tennis racquet ...51
tent ...33
theatre ...22
thermometer ...11
thin ...60
third ...59
thirteen ...57
thread ...43
three ...57
throwing ...54
thumb ...4
Thursday ...48
tiger ...40
tights ...7
time ...48
tins ...27
tissues ...17
toad ...32
toadstools ...35
toast ...15
toes ...5
toilet ...17
toilet rolls ...26
tomatoes ...14
toolbox ...20
toothbrush ...16
toothpaste ...16
top ...59
tortoise ...38

towel ...16
town hall ...22
toy car ...42
toy duck ...17
toy frog ...17
toy windmill ...46
tracksuit ...7
tractor ...36
trailer ...36
train ...31
train set ...42
trainers ...6
tree ...34
triangle ...44, 56
tricycle ...24
trolley ...27
trough ...36
trousers ...6
trowel ...18
trunk ...35, 41
Tuesday ...48
tulips ...19
tummy ...5
tummy button ...5
tusk ...41
twelve ...57
twenty ...57
twig ...34
two ...57
tyre ...28

Umbrella ...7
under ...59
up ...59

Vacuum cleaner ...10
valley ...32
van ...31
vegetable oil ...26
vegetables ...27
vest ...6
village ...32
vintage car ...29
violin ...44

Walking ...53
wall ...9
wallpaper ...8
wand ...55
wardrobe ...11
washbasin ...16
washing machine ...13
washing powder ...27
washing-up liquid ...26
wasp ...18
watch ...6
water ...16
water weed ...38
waterfall ...33
watering can ...19
waterlilies ...32
waves ...46
weather ...49
Wednesday ...48
weeds ...19
week ...48
weighing scales ...12
wellington boots ...7
wet ...60
wheel ...28
wheelbarrow ...19

whiskers ...38
whispering ...53
whistle ...42
white ...56
wild flowers ...33
window ...9
window box ...9
windowsill ...9
windscreen ...29
windscreen wipers ...29
wind ...49
wing ...28, 39
winter ...49
wires ...21
witch ...55
wizard ...55
wood ...20, 35
woodpecker ...35
woolly hat ...6
workbench ...20
worms ...19
wrench ...20
wrist ...4
writing ...45

Yacht ...51
year ...48
yellow ...56
yoghurt ...15

Zebra ...41

Additional Design
David Gillingwater, Mandy Earey
Additional Photography
Jo Foord, Steve Gorton, Paul Bricknell,
Philip Dowell, Michael Dunning,
Stephen Oliver, Steve Shott, Jerry Young

Dorling Kindersley would like to
thank Helen Drew and Brian Griver
for their help in producing this book,
and Leah Bellamy, Carmen Berzon,
Laura Douglas, Charlotte Harris, Holly
Jackman, Andrew Linnet, Paul Miller,
Robert Nagle, Hiral Patel, Sam Priddy,
Kayleigh Swan, George and Elizabeth
Wilkes, and Kimberley Yarde for
appearing in this book.